CONTENTS

IMAGES

My Body

Designed:
Émilie Beaumont

Text:
P. Simon

Pictures:
N. Soubrouillard

FLEURUS

ANATOMY

WE ARE ALL DIFFERENT

There are thousands of millions of human beings on the Earth but no one is exactly the same as anyone else.

We don't all have the same colour skin. Some of us are black or brown, others are white or yellow.

Even members of the same family don't look exactly alike. Everyone is different.

WE ARE ALL MADE IN THE SAME WAY

We can be tall or short, thin or fat, but we all have one head, two arms and two legs.

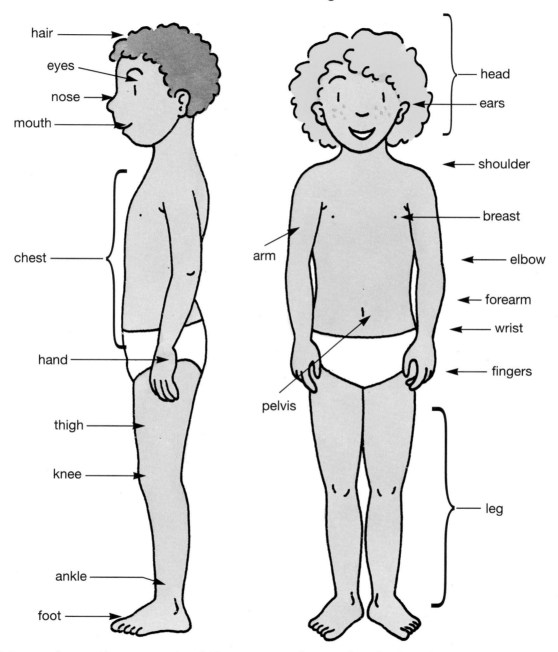

hair
eyes
nose
mouth
chest
hand
thigh
knee
ankle
foot

head
ears
shoulder
breast
elbow
forearm
wrist
fingers
leg

arm
pelvis

Point to and say the names of the parts of your body, beginning with your head.

9

THE SKELETON

Our bones help us to stand up, walk, run and dance. The body's bone structure is called the skeleton.

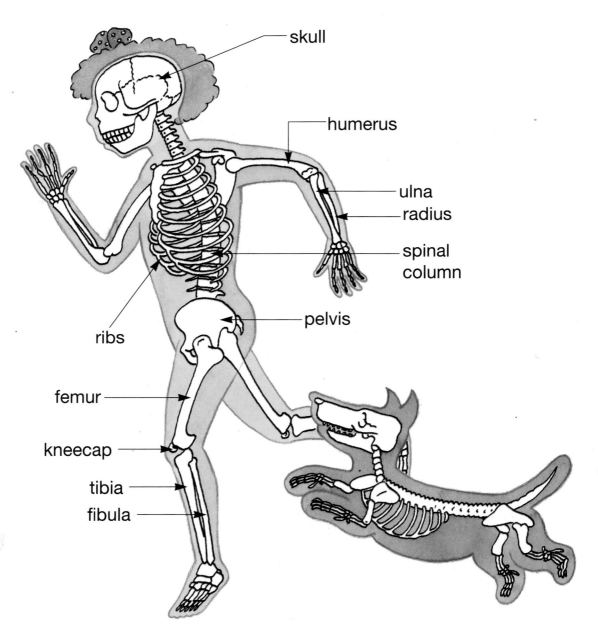

- skull
- humerus
- ulna
- radius
- spinal column
- pelvis
- ribs
- femur
- kneecap
- tibia
- fibula

The human body has 206 bones. These bones make up the skeleton and every bone has its own name. Try to learn the names of some of them.

DO ANIMALS HAVE SKELETONS?

Many animals have skeletons, including dogs, cats, birds, snakes and fish.

Animals with a skeleton are part of the family known as vertebrates. This means they have a spinal column.

Earthworms have no bones at all. Their bodies are completely soft.

Fish are vertebrates too, but their bones are much smaller than ours.

Crabs and snails have soft bodies which are protected by a hard shell outside. These animals belong to the family known as invertebrates, which means they do not have a spinal column.

BONES ARE NOT ALL THE SAME SHAPE

Bones can be long or short, tiny or large, or they can even be completely round.

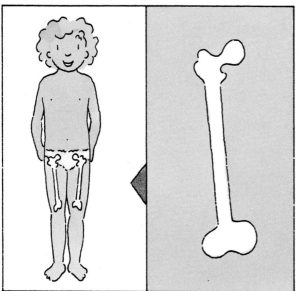

The femur or thigh bone is the longest bone in the body.

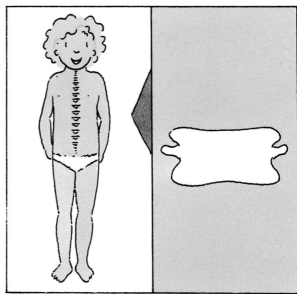

The spine is made up of lots of little bones called vertebrae.

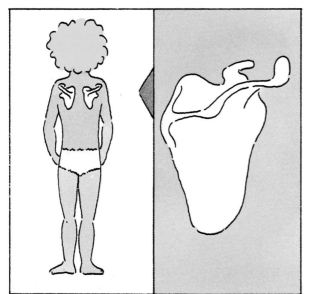

The scapula is a completely flat bone found in the shoulder.

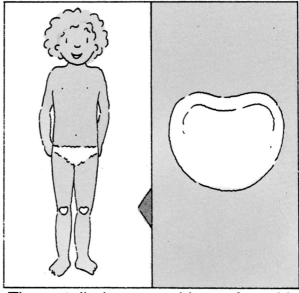

The patella is a round bone found in the knee.

WHAT USE ARE BONES?

Some organs in our bodies are very fragile. Bones, which are very tough, protect them from injury.

The skull protects the brain.

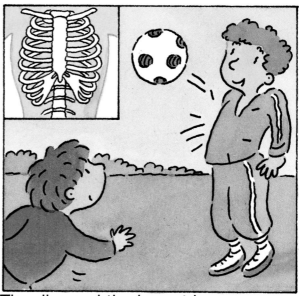

The ribs and the breast bone protect the heart and lungs.

If we didn't have bones, we couldn't stand up or even hold a pencil!

BONES GROW

Bones grow for twenty years, then they stop. That's why people stop getting taller when they are adults.

Babies are measured regularly to check their growth.

We need to eat well to make our bones grow.

Dwarves' bones stop growing too soon, while giants' bones have grown too much. Crocodiles' bones never stop growing!

BONES CAN MEND

Bones are tough but sometimes they break. We say that the bone has fractured.

This girl broke the bone in her arm when she fell off her skis.

In hospital, the doctor wraps her arm in plaster to keep it straight.

The bone takes a few weeks to mend.

At last the plaster is removed and her arm is completely healed.

HOW DOES THE SKELETON MOVE?

Bones are joined together by ligaments that help the bones move in many ways.

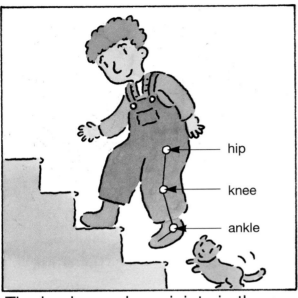

The leg bones have joints in three places.

Each finger is made up of three little bones.

The bones of the arm are joined in three places.

The lower jaw is the only bone in the skull that can move.

16

THE SPINAL COLUMN

If you run your hand down someone else's back you will feel a bumpy ridge that is the spinal column, or spine.

The spine is very supple. It enables us to roll forwards and backwards. The spine also holds up our head.

We can lean to the left or the right, but leaning backwards is more difficult. Try to get in the same position as this little boy.

CAN YOU DO THIS?

The body can move in many different ways, but can it really do everything?

Can you turn your head back to front, or can you lift up your leg like this boy?

Can you bend your leg in that direction, and can you turn the whole top half of your body back to front? I don't think so!

MUSCLES

Muscles are attached to our bones to enable us to lift up our arms, turn our heads, stoop down and stand up again.

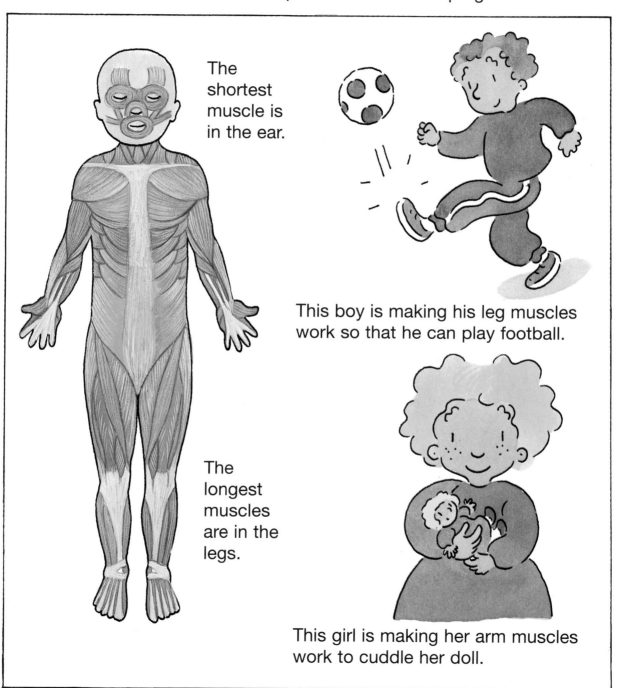

The shortest muscle is in the ear.

This boy is making his leg muscles work so that he can play football.

The longest muscles are in the legs.

This girl is making her arm muscles work to cuddle her doll.

WHY DO WE HAVE MUSCLES?

Muscles are long strips of fiber. Just like a piece of elastic, muscles stretch or shorten to make bones move.

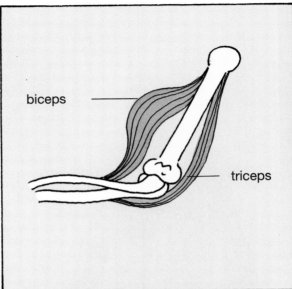

When the boy bends his arm, the biceps swells and pulls on the bone in the forearm. The triceps gets longer.

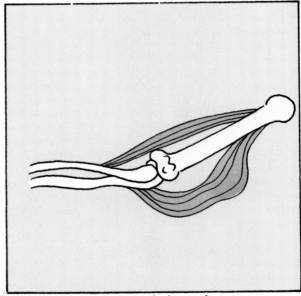

When he straightens his arm, the biceps gets longer and the triceps swells, pulling back the forearm bone. Touch one of your biceps as you bend your arm and you will feel the muscle working.

ALWAYS ACTIVE

There are many muscles in our bodies and they are always hard at work.

We laugh, we shout, we whistle, we close our eyes – our face muscles never stop working.

Blowing makes your chest muscles work.

Some diseases destroy muscles so they cannot work.

21

STRONG MUSCLES

Athletes train long and hard to develop powerful muscles.

The weight-lifter lifts heavy weights.

This cyclist is pedalling hard; his thigh muscles are very big.

Some people build up their muscles and enter contests to show them off.

There are machines to make our muscles work harder.

THE HEART

The heart is a very important organ. It is a muscle which never stops working, even at night. If the heart stops pumping, the body cannot live.

Your heart is about the same size as a clenched fist.

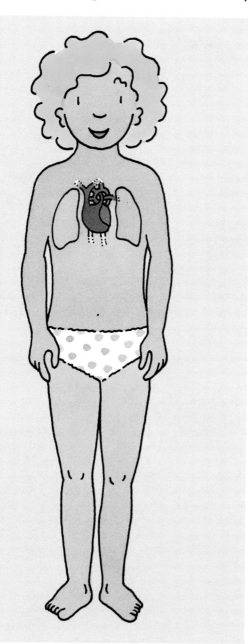

The heart is located between the lungs.

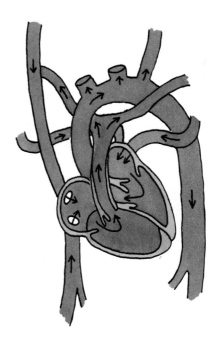

The heart first pumps blood through the lungs. Then the blood circulates around every part of the body before it returns to the heart.

THE HEARTBEAT

If you put your fingers on the veins in your wrist or your neck you can feel your heartbeat or pulse.

Try to feel your pulse in your wrist.

When we get up, the heart beats about 70 times a minute.

After a race the heart beats much faster.

When we are sick, the heart beats faster too.

BLOOD

Your body contains about three quarts of blood, while an adult's body has five quarts. Blood is a red liquid that is thicker than water.

Sometimes doctors have to take a blood sample.

The blood is examined under a microscope in a laboratory.

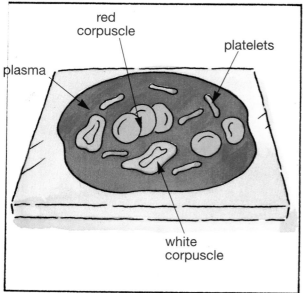

red corpuscle

platelets

plasma

white corpuscle

Blood is made up of many different elements.

People can give their blood to help save another person's life.

THE BLOOD CIRCULATION

Blood passes through thousands of miles of blood vessels to every part of the body.

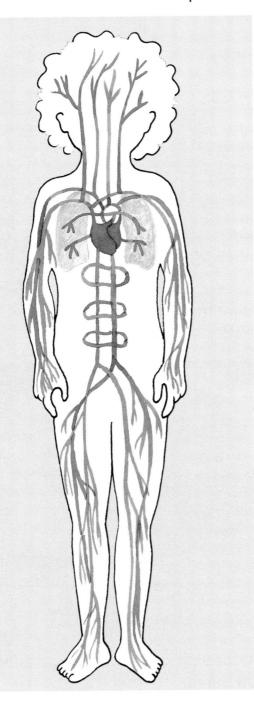

The blood carries red and white corpuscles and platelets throughout the body.

● The red corpuscles take oxygen from the lungs around the body. The carbon dioxide they pick up on their way is then expelled by the lungs.

● White corpuscles protect the body from germs.

● Platelets clot the blood when we cut ourselves.

● Blood flows very quickly. It leaves the heart through very large vessels called arteries and returns through other vessels called veins.

WHITE CORPUSCLES

White corpuscles are the body's defense against germs. Germs are too small to see, but they can still make us ill.

Germs are everywhere. They are in sand, in the earth, on plants, in food and in us – especially when we cough.

Animals carry germs too. We get many germs on our hands which is why we should always wash our hands before eating.

WE DON'T ALL HAVE THE SAME TYPE OF BLOOD

There are four blood groups: A, O, AB and B.
It is important to know which blood group we belong to.

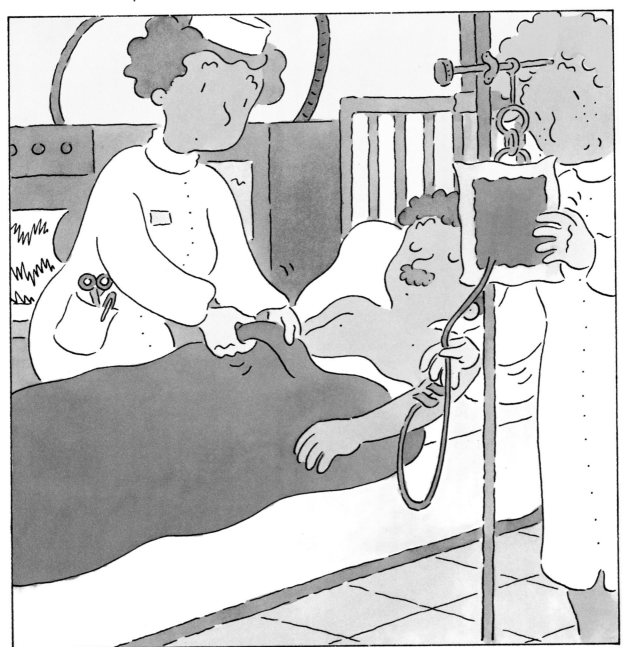

When a person has lost a lot of blood he is given a transfusion of another person's blood. He can only receive another person's blood if it will mix with his own.

WHAT ARE PLATELETS?

Platelets begin to work when a blood vessel is broken and blood begins to flow out of the body.

If you graze your knees, first you have to clean the wound. The platelets get to work to stop the blood flowing out and the germs getting in.

A hard crust forms which blocks up the wound.

When new skin forms, the wound is healed.

A HEALTHY HEART

The heart is like an engine. Without it the body cannot function, so we have to take good care of our heart.

We should not smoke because it causes heart disease. We should also watch what we eat, so we don't get too fat.

We should have regular exercise.

Doctors use an electrocardiogram to check the heart.

THE KIDNEYS

The kidneys get rid of waste material produced by the body. The blood carries the waste to the kidneys where the blood is cleaned.

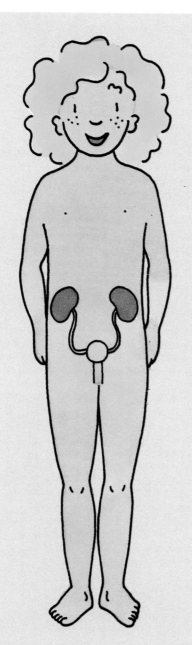

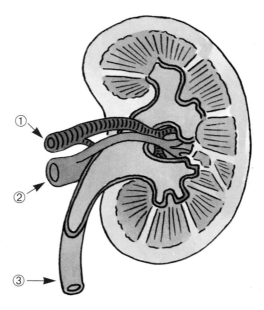

A kidney is shaped like a big bean and is just a little smaller than your fist. It is a very important organ because it keeps the blood clean. Inside are filters like little sieves which hold the waste products carried by the blood. This waste becomes urine which runs down to a container called the bladder.

1. and 2. Little tubes through which blood circulates.
3. Tube which carries urine to the bladder.

We have two kidneys. They are found on either side of the spine. Each kidney is linked to the bladder by a tube.

WHY DO WE NEED TO GO TO THE BATHROOM?

When the bladder is full of urine we have to empty it by going to the bathroom. If we don't, the bladder might overflow!

It's very hard to wait when we need to go to the toilet, so we should not wait too long between visits to the bathroom.

THE LUNGS

The lungs are located inside the rib cage. They have a very important job to do because they enable us to breathe.

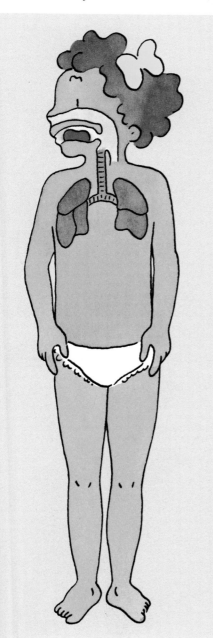

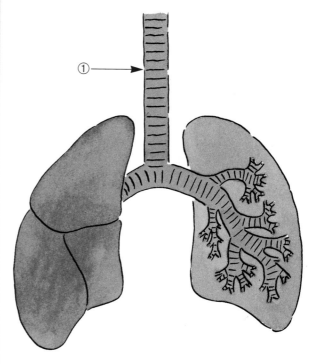

Picture of the lungs inside and outside.

1. The air which goes in and out of the lungs passes through this tube, which is called the trachea or windpipe.

Our brain and muscles need oxygen all the time. When the body has used this oxygen, a gas called carbon dioxide is produced which the body doesn't need. When we breathe, we are emptying our lungs of carbon dioxide and filling them with oxygen.

The first thing a baby does when it is born is to cry. This fills the lungs with air and the baby begins to breathe.

BREATHING

When we breathe, we fill our lungs with air which contains the oxygen that we need, and we expel the carbon dioxide.

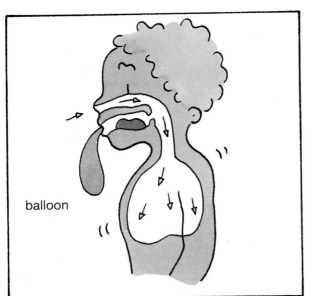

When we take in air, our lungs expand; the balloon remains flat. When we breathe out, we empty our lungs and the balloon fills with air.

In cold weather, the air we breathe out forms a little cloud.

Mountain climbers sometimes carry oxygen to help them breathe.

34

FAST AND SLOW BREATHING

We breathe all the time, but our breathing is faster or slower depending on what we are doing.

When we run, we need more oxygen so we breathe faster to get more air into our lungs.

When we walk, we breathe normally.

When we are asleep, our breathing is slow and regular.

HICCUPS

When we have hiccups, we aren't breathing normally.
The air goes out of our lungs very quickly with a funny noise.

We can get hiccups if we eat too quickly or swallow something that is too hot or too cold. The hiccups sometimes stop if we are frightened!

People say you can also stop hiccups by drinking a glass of water while holding your nose, or by holding your breath.

PROTECTING OUR LUNGS

Lungs are very fragile organs. The air that we breathe contains a lot of dust and many other particles.

Hairs inside the nose prevent dust from getting to the lungs.

Cigarette smoke contains tar which damages the lungs.

Some jobs create a lot of dust.

We should protect ourselves when there is too much dust in the air.

VOCAL CORDS

Vocal cords are two thin membranes in the throat which enable us to talk, shout and sing.

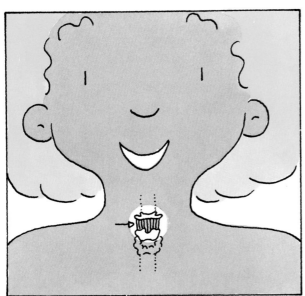 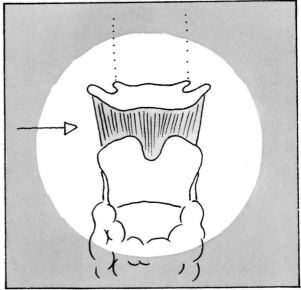

The vocal cords are at the bottom of the throat. When we speak, air passes over them producing the sound of our voice.

When boys are about 13 years old, their voices deepen.

No two voices are the same; we all sound different.

TEETH

Our teeth are set into our jaws. Teeth are very strong because they are covered by a very hard material called enamel.

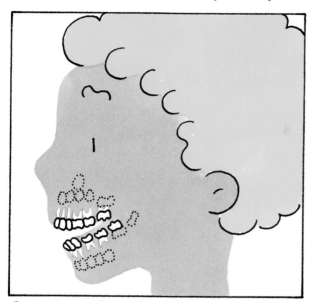

Our second teeth are below our baby teeth.

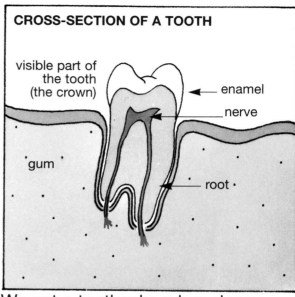

CROSS-SECTION OF A TOOTH

visible part of the tooth (the crown)

enamel

nerve

gum

root

We get a toothache when decay attacks the nerve.

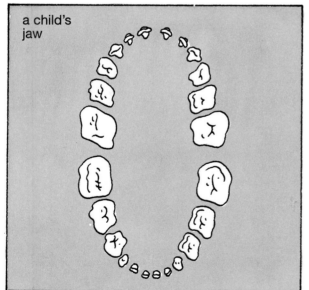

a child's jaw

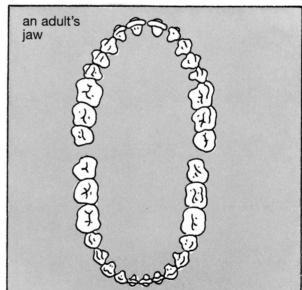

an adult's jaw

A child has 24 teeth; an adult has 32. The front teeth cut and tear the food and the big back teeth crush it.

BABY TEETH

Children have baby teeth until they are about six. We call them baby teeth because they come through when we are still babies.

Babies are born without any teeth.

The first teeth come through at about seven months.

Baby teeth begin to fall out from about the age of six.

Then the second teeth take their place.

THE STOMACH

We eat food to stay alive, but the body cannot make use of food in the form in which we eat it.

Our teeth cut and crush food to reduce it to a thick pulp. We then swallow this pulp down through the esophagus to the stomach.

The pulp stays in the stomach for several hours where it is digested. The stomach muscles act like a food mixer.

esophagus

stomach

WHY ARE WE HUNGRY?

The stomach is a big elastic pocket. When it is full of food, we are not hungry. When it's empty, we're hungry.

In the morning we're hungry: our stomach is empty.

We should always make time to eat a good breakfast.

All morning our stomachs are digesting the food.

By lunch time we are hungry again.

THE INTESTINES

By the time the food is ready to leave the stomach, it has become a very liquid pulp. It then goes into the intestines.

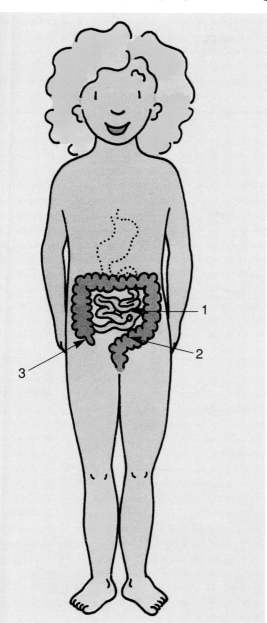

Sometimes the appendix (3) becomes infected and we have a very bad stomach-ache. We have to have a small operation to remove the appendix.

The small intestine separates what is good for our bodies and what is not. The useful products pass through the wall of the intestine and enter the blood. Waste products go into the large intestine and leave the body through the anus. These are the feces.

The intestines are in fact one very long tube going from the stomach to the anus.
1. small intestine 2. large intestine

STOMACH-ACHE

The stomach is a delicate organ. When we make it work too hard, it suffers and we get a stomach-ache.

If we eat too much, the stomach has difficulty in doing its job and we get a stomach-ache and feel sick.

We can also get stomach-ache if we eat too much between meals, or while we are playing.

44

FOOD HAS A LONG JOURNEY

Now you know what a long journey food makes through your body – but how much can you remember?

What happens to food in the mouth?

What does the stomach do with the food?

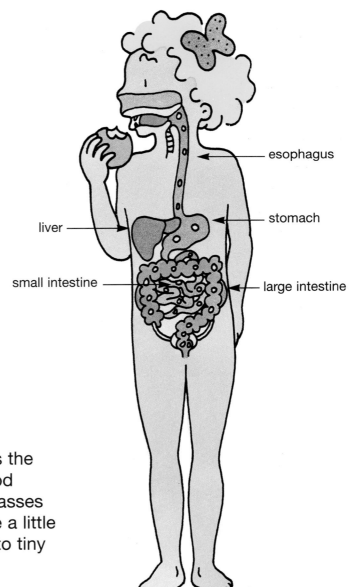

esophagus

stomach

liver

small intestine

large intestine

The liver: when blood leaves the small intestine it is full of good things for the body. It then passes through the liver which is like a little factory, transforming food into tiny particles.

The liver also produces bile which is a green liquid that helps digestion.

HOW IS THE UVULA USED?

The uvula (1) and the epiglottis (2) are little barriers which block the air passages to prevent food from getting into them.

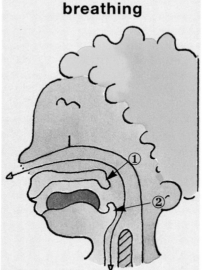

breathing   **swallowing**

The uvula can be seen at the back of the throat.

These pictures show the position of the uvula and the epiglottis when we breathe and when we swallow.

When we eat too quickly, the uvula and epiglottis don't always have time to shut off the passage to the lungs. Then we begin to cough and choke.

THE ORGANS GAME
Now you have learned about many organs in the body.
Can you recognize the ones drawn in the pictures below?

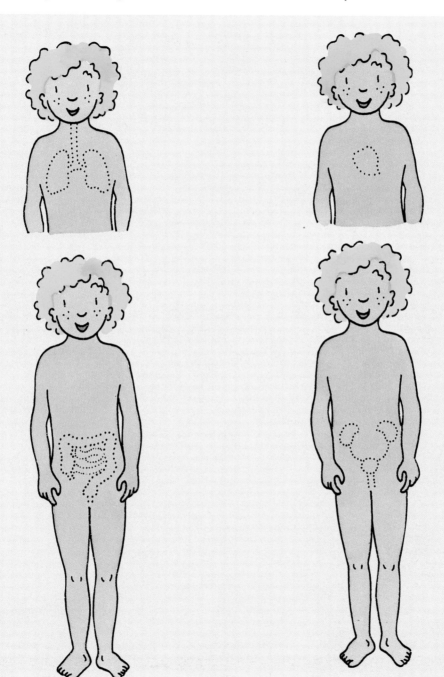

THE BRAIN – A WONDERFUL MACHINE

The brain is like a very powerful computer, working day and night.
The brain controls everything we do.

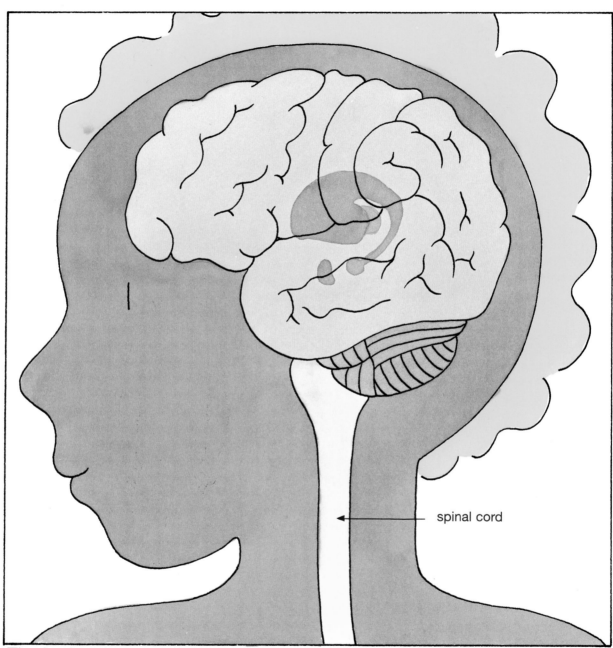

spinal cord

The brain takes up all the space inside the skull. It is joined to all the parts of the body by the spinal cord and the nerves.

THE NERVES

Nerves are like telephone wires. They link the brain to all parts of the body.

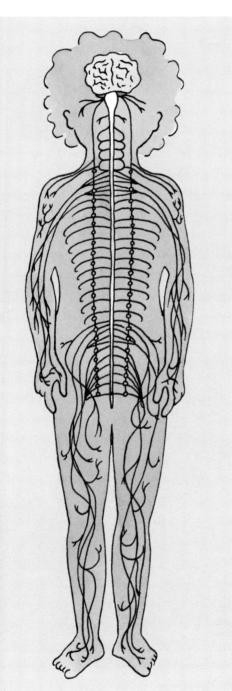

The brain is in charge of all your body's movements.

For example, when you hear the phone ring, little signals go along the nerve from your ear and alert your brain. If you decide to answer the phone, your brain sends orders to the muscles in your legs to make you stand up, and to the muscles in your hand to make you pick up the phone.

PINS AND NEEDLES

If we lean on nerves for too long, they can stop working properly.

When we sit like this, the nerves are squashed. They warn us that they have gone numb by producing pins and needles in our legs.

A gentle rub helps to bring back the feeling to the nerves.

If we carry a very heavy bag, our fingers go numb.

RIGHT- OR LEFT-HANDED

The brain decides which hand we use to hold a pen, scissors or a tennis racket.

The brain also decides which foot will be better at kicking the football.

Right-handed people find it easier to use their right hand than their left hand. Left-handers prefer to use the left.

THINKING

Every minute of the day we have to solve problems, think and make decisions.

This child has stopped in front of a fence. What will she do? She could go away again, climb over or go underneath.

She has made up her mind to crawl under.

Immediately, her brain tells her whole body what to do.

QUICK REACTIONS

Sometimes the brain makes decisions very quickly, and gives its orders before we have time to realize what is happening.

If we see danger approaching, we move to avoid it.

We might hear a very loud noise and shut our eyes.

The water is very cold so we quickly pull out our toes.

If we put something hot in our mouth, we spit it out.

MEMORY

Some pieces of information reach the brain then disappear. We forget them. Others stay in our memory and we remember them for a long time.

We need to learn certain precise movements to enable us to ride a bike. We never forget how to do this, even when we grow up.

We remember all sorts of things – a favorite toy, a house we once lived in, or an accident.

INTELLIGENCE

Our intelligence enables us to think, understand, find answers and learn new things.

Where do the missing squares go in this picture?

Which of these keys will open the box?

Put these apples in the right order. Think carefully!

Explain why the tree has fallen over.

DO YOU HAVE A GOOD MEMORY?

Look carefully at the pictures for about 20 seconds, then turn away and try to name all the red-colored objects.

You could have some fun by trying out this test on a grown-up. Count to 10 while they look, then ask them how many things they remember!

THE FIVE SENSES

TWO EYES TO SEE THE WORLD

Eyes are like camcorders. They take pictures which they immediately send to the brain.

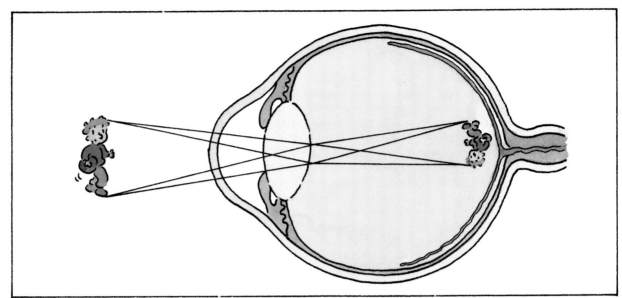

Light enters the eye, forming an image at the back of the eye. This image is upside down but the brain makes us see it the right way up.

Light enters the eye through a little opening called the pupil. In daylight the pupil is very small; in a dark cellar it is wide open.

THE EYES PROTECT THEMSELVES

Our eyes are very delicate but they have many efficient ways of protecting themselves.

When heat and air dry up the eyes, tears moisten them.

If dust gets into the eyes, tears wash it away.

Danger coming! The eyelids close, keeping the eyes safe.

When it rains, the eyebrows and eyelashes keep the rain off.

WHO NEEDS GLASSES?

Some people don't see very well. Their eyes make blurred images.
Glasses help the eyes to make clear images.

This little girl is shortsighted. She cannot see things properly if they are
too far away. Her glasses enable her to read the stop sign clearly.

Grandma cannot see things that are close to her. She has to hold her
newspaper away to read it. Her glasses enable her to read it easily.

WHY DO WE HAVE TWO EYES?

Having two eyes allows us to see many things around us without turning our heads.

Try this. Look straight in front of you and push your arms backwards. How far back can you see them? Now close one eye. What happens?

Our eyes help us keep our balance too. Try to stand on one leg with both your eyes open. Then close one eye – you'll find it's more difficult!

EARS

Ears have a special shape, like a shell, which helps us hear well.

If you put your hand behind your ear, you hear better.

Even blindfolded we know where noise is coming from.

The inner part of the ear is very important. It transmits sounds to the brain to be recognized.

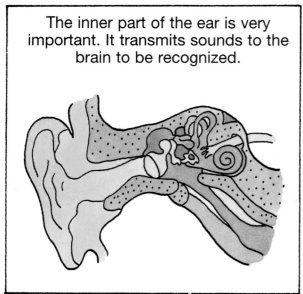

The visible, outer part of the ear is called the pinna.

If a child's ears stick out, we should not make fun of him.

THE EARDRUM

The eardrum is a small, thin piece of skin, like the skin of a drum.
It vibrates when sounds enter the ear.

The ear produces a yellow, sticky paste we call ear-wax to protect the
eardrum. It stops dust from getting in. You might see it on a cotton-swab.

When we climb mountains, the air inside the ear puts pressure on the
eardrum and the ear pops. We can't hear very well. When we go back
down the mountain, we can hear as well as before.

BEWARE NOISE!

Very loud noises can damage the inner ear and cause deafness, so we have to be careful when there is a lot of noise.

People doing certain jobs have to wear ear-muffs to protect themselves against the noise.

You shouldn't play the music too loud on your personal stereo.

Don't stand too near a drummer.

BALANCE

The inner part of the ear enables us to keep our balance.

When we are in danger of falling over, the inner ear warns the brain. The brain then orders our muscles to move so that we keep our balance.

Cars and boats shake us around. These movements make us sea-sick or car-sick because they disturb the inner ear, which keeps our balance.

BLIND AND DEAF

If we cannot see, we are blind.
If we cannot hear, we are deaf.

A blind man uses a white stick when he goes out. He moves it in front of his body to help him avoid obstacles. He could also use a guide-dog.

Blind people use their fingers to read books in Braille.

Deaf people cannot always speak. They use sign language.

THE SKIN

The skin is like a tough elastic envelope which covers our body.
On the surface are little holes called pores.

As we get older, our skin changes and wrinkles appear.

Skin is elastic. It stretches as the stomach gets fatter.

Skin contains melanin, which gives it color. The more melanin in the skin, the darker the color. Less melanin means lighter color.

FRECKLES AND BEAUTY SPOTS

Light-skinned people often have little dark spots on the skin called freckles.

Freckles are darker in the summer because of the sun.

If we are born with beauty spots, they won't disappear.

A baby's skin color depends on its parents. Light skins are usually more delicate than dark skins.

BEWARE OF THE SUN

Skin protects itself from the sun's rays by producing a large amount of melanin. The skin gets darker and we have a suntan.

If we stay in the sun too long, the skin burns. It dies and comes off – we peel. In a few days, new skin appears.

When we get hot, we perspire.

Sweat runs out of the pores and cools us.

GOOSEBUMPS

When it gets cold, the skin reddens, the hairs stand up and we shiver.
We have goosebumps.

The erect hairs close the pores so that heat stays inside the body.

We shiver, making our muscles move quickly so that we warm up.

Sometimes a bad scare can give us goosebumps.

When the scare is over, the pores open up and we sweat.

GETTING OUT OF THE BATH TUB

The skin on the palms of our hands and the soles of our feet is thicker than anywhere else. If we stay in the tub for a long time, our skin wrinkles.

While we're in the tub, the skin swells up with water like a sponge.

It becomes soft and squashy.

Our nails become softer too. If we need to cut our nails, this is the time to do it because it's much easier.

NAILS AND FINGERPRINTS

The skin at the end of our fingers and toes is protected on one side by the nails. The other side is ridged with little lines called fingerprints.

Fingerprints help us to hold objects without letting them slip. We have these prints at the ends of our fingers and under our feet.

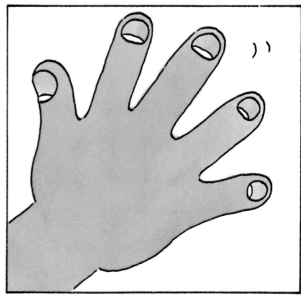

We all have fingerprints, but nobody has the same prints as anybody else.

Children's nails grow faster than adults' nails.

BODY HAIR

We think that the first men and women on Earth had thick hair all over their bodies which protected them from the cold.

Our bodies are covered with hair too, except on the lips, on the palm of the hand and under the feet. As we grow older we get more hair.

Animal hair is thicker and tougher than ours.

Men have more hair than women.

MORE THAN 80,000 HAIRS

Hair is like a hat, a bonnet or an umbrella. It protects the head from the cold, from the sun's rays and the rain.

Blond, brown, red or chestnut – the color of our hair depends on the amount of melanin in our bodies.

SKIN IS SENSITIVE

When we touch something, our skin sends information to the brain.
We then know if something is warm, cold or smooth.

The most sensitive parts of the body are the lips, the hands and the feet.

Some parts of the body react to being tickled and make us laugh.
Where are you ticklish?

RECOGNIZING WHAT WE TOUCH

Our skin helps us know if something is cold, hot, dry or wet.

We also recognize what feels nice, what hurts, what is hard and what's soft.

Sometimes the skin gets confused. If you put your hand into iced water, then into cold water, the cold water will feel warm!

THE TONGUE

Each part of the tongue recognizes a different taste except for the center, which doesn't recognize any tastes at all.

The back of the tongue recognizes bitter tastes, like onions.

The tongue also feels heat, cold and pain (when you bite your tongue, for example).

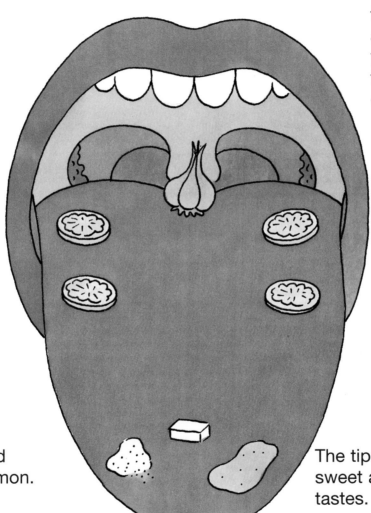

The sides recognize acid tastes, like lemon.

The tip recognizes sweet and spicy tastes.

If you burn your tongue on something very hot, you won't be able to taste anything properly for a few days.

77

SALIVA

To be able to recognize the taste of food, the tongue must always be moistened by saliva.

If your tongue is dry, you'll find it harder to taste things. Try this: dry your tongue and then eat a bit of sugar.

We make more saliva when we are about to eat something we really like.

It's difficult to taste anything with the underside of the tongue.

THE NOSE

The nose smells scents in the air. Little tubes link the nose to the ears and the eyes.

All noses are different shapes. This is what gives personality to our faces.

WHY DOES THE NOSE RUN?

When we have a cold, the skin inside the nose dries out. To make this better, the nose produces a liquid which runs out of our nostrils.

Our noses often run in the winter.

Sometimes we use nose drops to clear the nose.

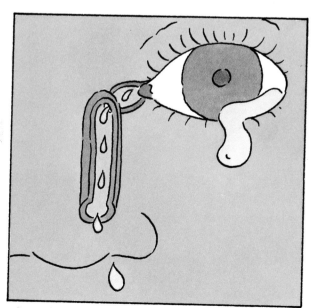

A very short tube links the eyes to the nose. When we start to cry, the nose begins to run.

RECOGNIZING SMELLS

It is very important to be able to recognize smells. The smell of gas means danger. If a fish smells bad, we don't eat it.

Even blindfolded we recognize smells.

When we have a cold, we can hardly smell anything.

Very strong smells can make us feel sick.

Some people work with smells to create perfume.

TRUE OR FALSE?

Now you have learned a lot more about your body, but how much can you remember? Answer true or false to the following questions.

1. The femur is a bone.

2. We keep our baby teeth until we are 20.

3. Our ears help us keep our balance.

4. If we stay in the water too long, our skin gets covered in spots.

5. The brain helps with digestion.

BIRTH AND GROWING UP

WANTING A BABY

Lucy's parents love each other very much and hope to make Lucy a little brother or sister.

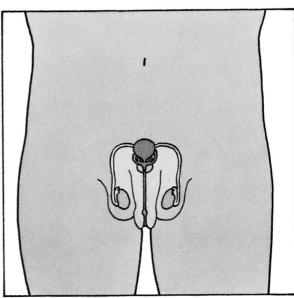

To make the baby they tenderly hold each other close.

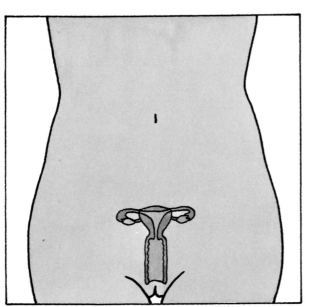
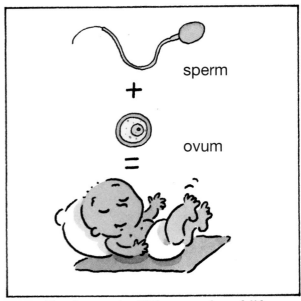

sperm

ovum

When they are both feeling great pleasure, Dad sends little seeds of life, called sperm, into Mom's stomach. Mom has a seed of life inside her, called an ovum.

THE BEGINNINGS OF LIFE

To make a baby, one of Dad's sperm must find Mom's ovum.
This is called fertilizing the egg.

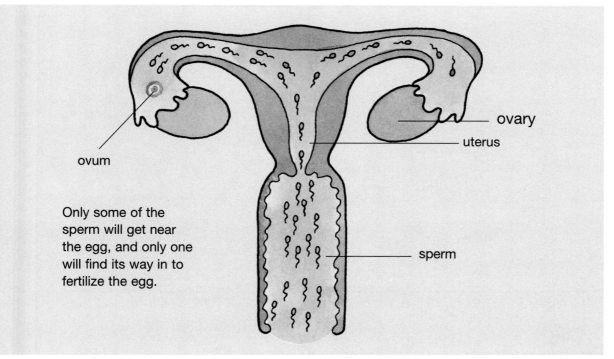

ovum

ovary

uterus

sperm

Only some of the
sperm will get near
the egg, and only one
will find its way in to
fertilize the egg.

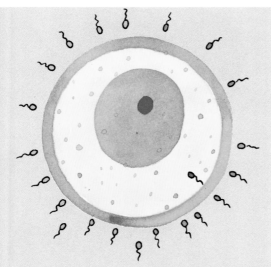

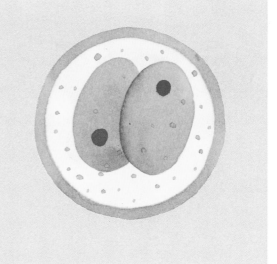

Several hours after it has been fertilized, the egg begins to divide.
The sperm that did not reach the egg, die.

A NEST FOR THE EGG

A new life has begun, but Mom does not know that yet. She has to have some tests.

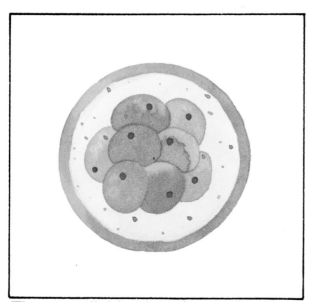

The egg divides into four cells, then into eight.

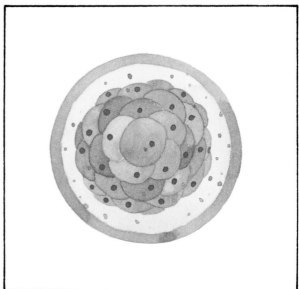

Within a few days, hundreds of cells have been formed.

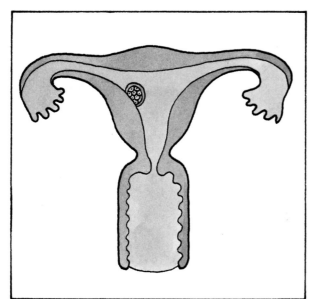

The egg settles down in the uterus, where it will grow.

Mom has the results of her tests. She is pregnant.

THE FIRST MONTHS

These are very important months because the egg is changing and turning into a tiny baby.

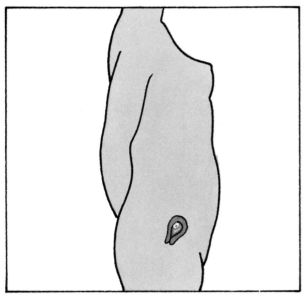

At the end of the first month, the baby's heart begins to beat.

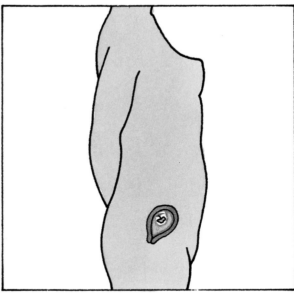

By the third month, important body parts have been formed.

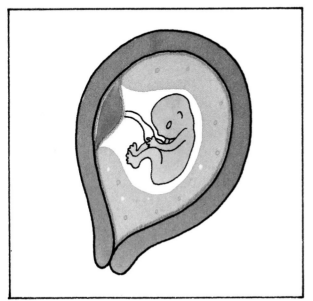

Enlarged view of a baby at two months.

Mom often feels sick and she's very tired.

THIRD AND FOURTH MONTHS

The baby's inner organs are now complete, but very tiny. Now the rest of the baby can grow.

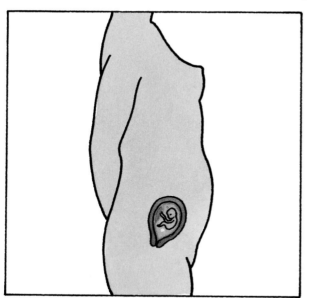

At three months, the fingers and toes are formed.

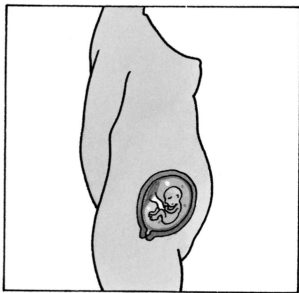

At four months, the baby begins to move and its hair grows.

During her pregnancy, Mom watches her weight carefully and often goes to the doctor to make sure that everything is going well.

SIXTH AND SEVENTH MONTHS

The baby gets bigger and bigger. It can suck its thumb and kick its legs inside Mom's stomach.

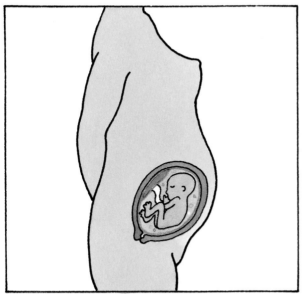

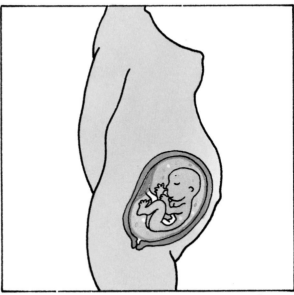

At six months, the baby can cross its arms.

At seven months, the baby can hear its mother's voice.

Mom's stomach has grown big and round. It is time to buy clothes for the baby. Lucy chooses the pajamas.

THE LAST MONTHS

At the end of the ninth month, Mom begins to feel pains in her stomach. Baby will be born soon.

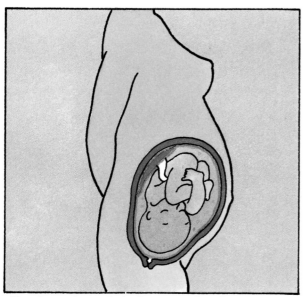

During the eighth month, the baby turns head down.

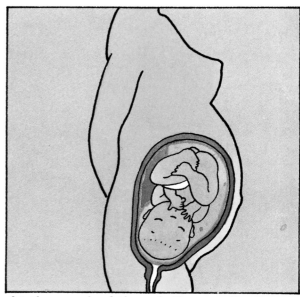

At the end of the ninth month, the baby will leave the warm nest.

Mom's stomach is enormous.

Everything is ready for the baby. Mom goes off to hospital.

THE GREAT DAY

The baby has spent nine months growing inside Mom's stomach.
Now the baby is ready to be born.

It's a boy! He is put onto Mom's stomach. Dad is very happy because he watched his son being born.

THE UMBILICAL CORD

While the baby was inside Mom's stomach, he received everything he needed through this little tube.

After the birth, the doctor cuts the cord to separate the baby from his mother.

The belly button shows where the cord was attached.

We have to make sure that we keep our belly button nice and clean.

THE FIRST MOMENTS OF LIFE

When the baby is born, he is washed by a nurse.

The baby begins to cry, which helps his lungs to work.

Then the baby is cleaned, measured and weighed.

A little identity bracelet is put around his wrist.

The baby doesn't eat food at first – he only drinks milk.

TWINS

Sometimes a mother gives birth to two babies at the same time.
These are twins.

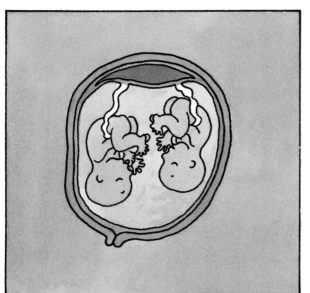

If the egg inside Mom has divided in two, the two babies are identical twins. They look exactly like each other.

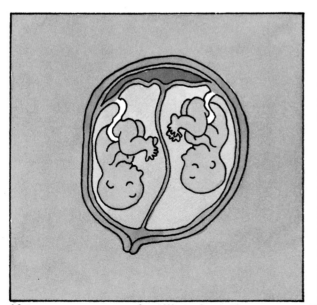

If two eggs are fertilized at the same time, the two babies are not identical twins. They are not exactly like each other.

BATHING THE BABY

Some parts of a newborn baby's body are very delicate. We must take great care when we bath him.

The head is fragile; the bones have not set properly yet.

The belly button needs a lot of care.

Powder keeps the skin dry and soft.

Now the baby can be dressed.

THE BABY IS CRYING

A newborn baby cannot talk, so he cries to call his mother. But his body is not able to make tears yet.

The baby cries when he is hungry, day and night.

He cries when he's too cold or when he's too hot.

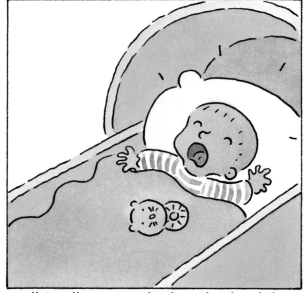

He cries when he's tired, when he has a dirty diaper and when he is sick.

THE BABY IS GROWING

During the first months of his life, the baby grows very quickly. He soon begins to notice the world around him.

At about two months, the baby smiles for the first time.

At four months, he begins to eat solid food.

At six months, he can sit up and take hold of his toys.

His first teeth come through. These are his baby teeth.

THE BABY LEARNS TO WALK

Baby animals can walk as soon as they are born. A human baby has to wait until he is about one, perhaps older, before he can walk on his own.

At birth, the doctor does a walking test on the baby.

At seven or eight months, the baby learns to crawl.

At around one year, he can stand up alone and walk without help. But he is not very sure of himself and often falls.

CHILDHOOD

With the help of his parents, his brothers and sisters, and later by going to school, the young child learns many difficult things.

At about two, the baby can usually speak properly.

At three, he is toilet-trained and can go to nursery school.

From the age of four, he can control all his movements. He can eat alone, get dressed, brush his hair and clean his teeth.

ELEMENTARY SCHOOL

At about five, the child begins elementary school. This is a very important stage in childhood.

At school, he will begin to learn to read, write and do math.

At seven, his baby teeth begin to fall out.

By the age of eight, he has learned all sorts of skills. He loves to have fun with his friends.

ADOLESCENCE

A child's body changes as it grows. A boy turns into a man, and a girl turns into a woman. This is called adolescence.

From about 13 years old, a boy's shoulders grow wider, his voice deepens and hair appears on his face, his chest and under his arms. His personality changes too!

ADOLESCENCE IN GIRLS

From about 11 years old, a girl's body begins to change.

Her breasts begin to grow.

Hair grows under her arms.

She likes to spend time with her friends. Her personality changes.

She doesn't always agree with her parents.

ADULTHOOD

At about age 20, the body stops growing. It won't get any taller, but the muscles continue to develop.

Between 20 and 30, the male body becomes more muscular.

Between 30 and 40, people put on weight more easily.

Between 40 and 50, some men begin to lose their hair.

From about age 60, the hair turns white and the body thickens.

103

OLD AGE

In old age, bones become more fragile and muscles less powerful.
The skin on the face becomes wrinkled.

Old people often wear glasses because the eyes can't see so well.

They sometimes need a stick to help them walk.

But some elderly people still like to take a lot of exercise.

People can live for a long time – sometimes more than 100 years!

FOOD AND HYGIENE

EATING WELL

Most of us enjoy eating. Eating well means having a balanced diet and not eating too much.

Food is made up of many different elements and our bodies need all of them. To be really healthy, we need a little of each element.

ENERGY-GIVING FOODS

Sugars and fats give the body the energy it needs to work well.

We find sugars in bread, pasta, potatoes and beans (or vegetables).
We find fats in meat, oil, milk and butter.

We don't need the same amount of sugars and fats in one day.
The amount we need depends on our age and how active we are.

FOODS WHICH HELP US TO GROW

All sorts of different foods are necessary if the body is to grow.

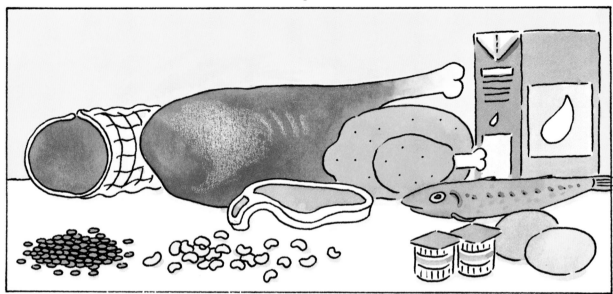

Meat, fish, eggs, milk and vegetables are all important foods for growth.

The baby gets everything he needs to grow in his baby food.

If you have been injured, food helps the body to heal.

VITAMINS

Vitamins are substances found in all foods. They help all the organs, including the heart, liver and eyes, to work well.

The vitamins we get from fruit and vegetables help us to fight off illness.

The vitamins we get from oily fish, cheese and butter strengthen the bones.

The vitamins in liver, butter, eggs and oil are good for the eyes and the skin.

Vitamins found in meat, cereals, fruit and vegetables are good for the muscles.

WHY SHOULD WE EAT?

We eat to keep our bodies going, and to give us enough energy to enjoy our daily activities.

After a long night without eating, your body needs food so that you can work well at school.

We have to eat to grow.

We also eat to keep us warm.

HOW SHOULD WE EAT?

The stomach needs lots of energy to digest the food we eat. If that energy is used up by the other organs, the stomach gets tired.

We shouldn't argue while we are eating.

We shouldn't play while we're eating, nor immediately afterwards.

We shouldn't eat between meals because it tires the stomach.

After a meal we should rest quietly for a while.

111

A BALANCED MEAL

A balanced meal should include meat or fish with vegetables,
a yogurt or cheese, and a pudding.

A meal of:
– fried egg
– chips
– cake

A meal of:
– a chicken leg
– 2 slices of meat
– cake
– ice-cream

A meal of:
– chopped raw vegetables
– meat and vegetables
– yogurt
– fruit

A meal of:
– hamburger
– hot dog
– sweets
– cake

Only one of the above menus will give you a well-balanced meal.
Which one? What is wrong with the other meals?

WE ALL NEED SLEEP

During the day we use up a lot of energy. At night our body is tired.
When we are little, we need to sleep a lot.

We yawn and rub our eyes.
This is a sign that we are sleepy.

We don't always want to go to bed,
even when we are tired.

We like to have a teddy bear or
something else close to us.

We like it when Dad or Mom reads
us a story.

DREAMS

The brain rests at night too, but not all the time. About every two hours it starts to work again and we dream.

We dream about what we have done or seen during the day.

We dream about something we would really like to have.

Sometimes we have very strange dreams.

And sometimes we talk about our dreams while we're asleep!

We dream more than once every night, but we don't always remember our dreams.

Sometimes we dream of scary things. These are nightmares.

When we wake up after a nightmare, it is hard to go back to sleep.

Sleepwalkers get up, walk around and then go back to bed while they are asleep. When they wake up, they don't remember anything about it.

TAKING CARE OF OURSELVES WHEN WE'RE SICK

Sometimes we don't feel very well and we have a high temperature.
The doctor comes to see us, or perhaps we go to his office.

The doctor looks for lumps in the neck.

He listens to our breathing with a stethoscope.

He looks at the back of our throat.

He makes sure we don't have a stomach-ache.

When the doctor has finished his examination, he often knows what is wrong with us and can make us better.

He writes out a prescription for the medicine to buy at the drugstore.

The medicine helps the body to fight the illness.

Sometimes we have to go to hospital to get better.

ILLNESS

When we are young, we often get illnesses which give us a high temperature and spots. We have to stay in bed.

Chicken-pox gives us some very itchy spots.

Mumps makes our cheeks hurt and swell.

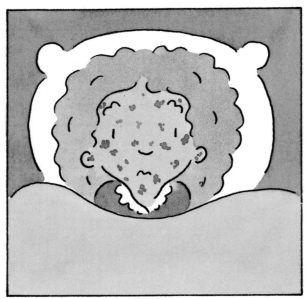

Measles gives us red spots all over our body.

In winter we often catch colds and then we cough a lot.

VACCINES

Sometimes we have to go to the doctor to be vaccinated. This protects us from getting some very serious illnesses.

Unfortunately, we don't have vaccines against all diseases, but scientists work hard every day trying to discover new vaccines.

119

SERIOUS ILLNESS

Cancer is a serious disease which can stop the body from working properly, so it needs to be treated.

The treatment of cancer can cause hair loss.

Sometimes a scanner is used to look inside the body.

Sometimes an operation is necessary to cure certain illnesses.

After a very serious illness we usually have to rest.

BUMPS AND BRUISES

Sometimes we give ourselves a nasty bump which doesn't break the skin. The blood vessels open and the blood flows under the skin.

If you bump an arm or a leg, a little pool of blood forms under the skin, making a bruise.

If you bang your head, you get a lump. Then you have to press something cold on it. Be careful not to rub it.

WHY SHOULD WE WASH?

We perspire all the time, even at night. When sweat dries, it begins to smell unpleasant, so we have to wash to smell nice.

A shower in the morning wakes us up. At night, a bath relaxes us, making the body ready for a good night's sleep.

Washing gets rid of any germs on our body which could make us ill.

Sometimes we have a sponge bath instead of a shower or a regular bath.
Afterwards we need to dry ourselves thoroughly with a towel.

We should regularly use a nail brush to keep our nails nice and clean.
A pumice stone gets rid of the dead skin on our feet.

HAIRCARE

Hair lives for four or five years, then it falls out and other hair grows in its place.

We should wash our hair with a gentle shampoo.

Hair breaks if it grows too long, so we should have it trimmed regularly.

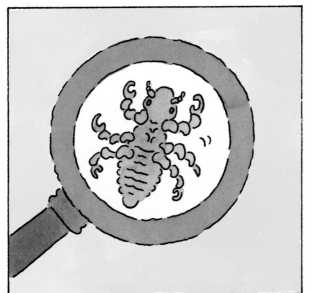

Sometimes we get small insects in our hair called lice. Special shampoo and regular combing will get rid of them.

HOW IS OUR HAIR USEFUL?

We should take good care of our hair because it has a very important job to do: it protects our head.

Hair stops the sun's rays from burning the skin on our head.

Hair protects our head from the cold.

Hair cushions our head from a blow.

Our hair is all different colors and shapes.

HEALTHY TEETH

It is easy to have healthy teeth if we look after them.

Brush your teeth daily, and after every meal.

Eat eggs, fish, cheese, and drink milk.

Don't strain your teeth by biting things you shouldn't eat.

Visit the dentist for a check-up twice a year.

TOOTH DECAY

If you don't clean your teeth, bits of food will get stuck between them. Then germs will develop and cause tooth decay.

If you get a toothache when you eat ice-cream, you might have some tooth decay. Go to the dentist.

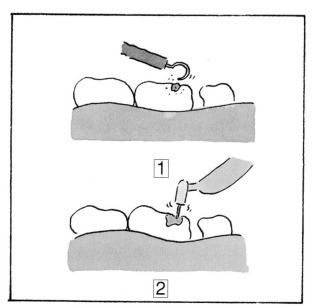 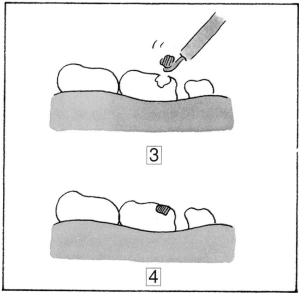

1. The dentist gets rid of the decay from the hole. 2. He cleans the hole with the drill. 3. He fills the hole with dental cement. 4. The filling is complete.

EXERCISE

It is very important to exercise to stay in good shape and in good health.

Sports help to make our muscles strong.

Sports also help to develop the heart and the lungs.

Running uses up a lot of energy, which is good if we are too fidgety.

It's fun to play together with our family or with friends.

ANGER AND HUGS

When we are very upset, we get angry. Afterwards we need a big hug from someone we love.

When something upsets us, we sometimes get angry.

We shout and cry, and our heartbeat gets faster.

We stamp our feet and get very excited.

A hug helps us to calm down and forget all about it.

LAUGHING AND CRYING

We laugh when we are happy and cry when we are sad. It's not only children who laugh and cry – grown-ups do it too.

We laugh when we see or hear something funny.

When we laugh, our cheek muscles relax and we open our mouth wide.

We cry when we are hurt or when we are sad. Our eyes fill with tears which run down our cheeks.

TRUE OR FALSE?

Now you know a lot about the human body. See how much you can remember and answer true or false to the following questions.

1. Food goes into the lungs.

2. The liver beats 70 times per minute.

3. We breathe more slowly when we are asleep.

4. Our bones grow throughout our whole lives.

5. We all have the same fingerprints at the end of our fingers.

6. Blood is made up of white corpuscles and yellow corpuscles.

7. Adults have 32 teeth.